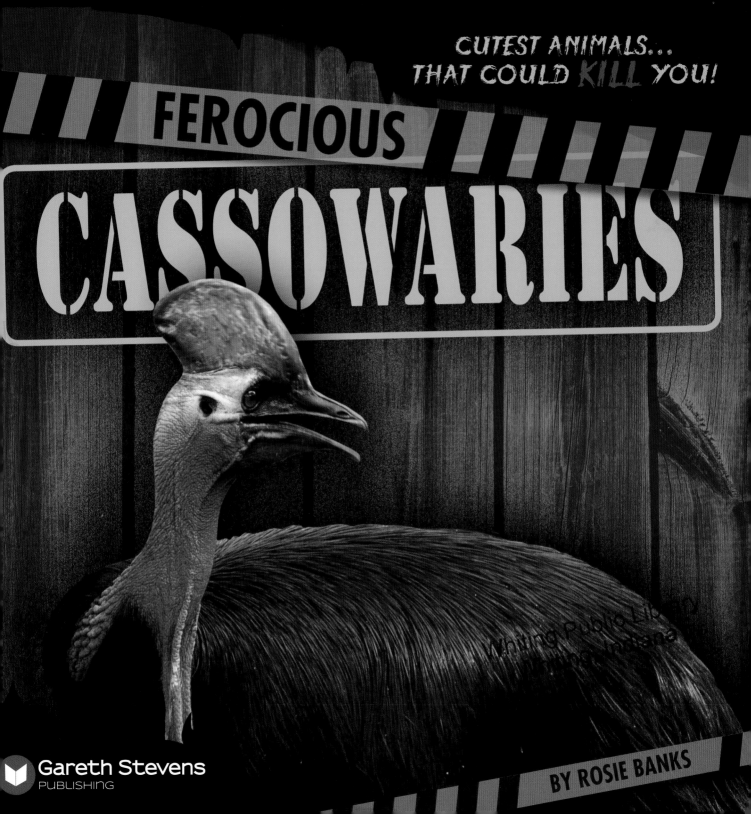

CUTEST ANIMALS...
THAT COULD **KILL** YOU!

FEROCIOUS
CASSOWARIES

Gareth Stevens
PUBLISHING

BY ROSIE BANKS

Please visit our website, www.garethstevens.com. For a free color catalog of all our high-quality books, call toll free 1-800-542-2595 or fax 1-877-542-2596.

Cataloging-in-Publication Data

Names: Banks, Rosie.
Title: Ferocious cassowaries / Rosie Banks.
Description: New York : Gareth Stevens Publishing, 2018. | Series: Cutest animals...that could kill you! | Includes index.
Identifiers: ISBN 9781538210840 (pbk.) | ISBN 9781538210864 (library bound) | ISBN 9781538210857 (6 pack)
Subjects: LCSH: Ratites–Juvenile literature.
Classification: LCC QL676.2 B36 2018 | DDC 598.5–dc23

First Edition

Published in 2018 by
Gareth Stevens Publishing
111 East 14th Street, Suite 349
New York, NY 10003

Designer: Sarah Liddell
Editor: Therese Shea

Photo credits: Cover, p. 1 Worakit Sirijinda/Shutterstock.com; wood texture used throughout Imageman/Shutterstock.com; slash texture used throughout d1sk/Shutterstock.com; pp. 4–5 Wendy Townrow/Shutterstock.com; p. 7 (southern cassowary) Marius Dobilas/Shutterstock.com; p. 7 (northern cassowary) VladSer/Shutterstock.com; p. 7 (dwarf cassowary) ZSSD/Minden Pictures/Minden Pictures/Getty Images; p. 7 (map) AridOcean/Shutterstock.com; p. 9 Barcroft/Contributor/Barcroft Media/Getty Images; p. 11 Pe3k/Shutterstock.com; p. 13 Andrea Izzotti/Shutterstock.com; p. 14 Kevin Schafer/Minden Pictures/Minden Pictures/Getty Images; p. 15 Auscape/Universal Images Group/Getty Images; p. 16 HTO/Wikimedia Commons; p. 17 Martin Willis/Minden Pictures/Minden Pictures/Getty Images; pp. 18–19 icosha/Shutterstock.com; p. 21 Artemii Sanin/Shutterstock.com.

Printed in China

CPSIA compliance information: Batch #CW18GS: For further information contact Gareth Stevens, New York, New York at 1-800-542-2595.

CONTENTS

Words in the glossary appear in **bold** type the first time they are used in the text.

FIGHT, BUT NO FLIGHT

It's strange to think of a bird as dangerous. But what if the bird was as big as you? And what if it had a supersharp claw on each foot? You'd probably stay far away—and you should!

Cassowaries are large, flightless birds that live in Australia and some islands around it. They have a bright blue head. You might want to pet a cute cassowary, but that's a bad idea. They can really hurt people!

5

THREE SPECIES

There are three species, or kinds, of cassowaries. The common, or southern, cassowary lives in Australia, New Guinea, and nearby islands. It's the largest of the three species and can be more than 5 feet (1.5 m) tall! The northern cassowary is just a bit smaller. It's native to New Guinea's northern **lowlands**.

The dwarf cassowary is the smallest species and can be 3.5 feet (1.1 m) tall. It lives in the **highlands** of New Guinea and on the island of New Britain.

THE DANGEROUS DETAILS

The cassowary is the second-heaviest bird in the world. Only the ostrich is heavier. Female southern cassowaries can weigh almost 130 pounds (59 kg).

CASSOWARY
TERRITORY

FEMALE CASSOWARIES
ARE USUALLY BIGGER
THAN THE MALES.

ASIA

NEW
GUINEA

NEW
BRITAIN

AUSTRALIA

ANTARCTICA

WHERE CASSOWARIES LIVE

SOUTHERN
CASSOWARY

DWARF
CASSOWARY

NORTHERN
CASSOWARY

7

FOREST BIRDS

People have found it hard to study cassowaries because the birds live in thick **rainforests**. When they spot people, they run away. However, scientists think the birds are most active at sunrise and sunset. This is when they look for food.

Cassowaries mostly eat fruit. They also eat some animals, such as frogs, birds, mice, bugs, and carrion—dead meat! They even eat soil sometimes. Scientists think they do this because soil has **minerals** that they don't get in other foods.

THE DANGEROUS DETAILS

The cassowary's big body and small wings are covered by thick, black feathers. They keep the bird dry in the wet rainforest. They also keep it from being cut by thorny plants.

9

CASQUE AND WATTLE

Cassowaries look different from the birds you see in your neighborhood. They have a casque (KASK) on the top of their head. It's made of **spongy** matter, but is covered with keratin, which is the same material that makes up your fingernails.

Southern cassowaries have two wattles. A wattle is a bare piece of skin that hangs from the neck of some birds. Northern cassowaries have one wattle, and dwarf cassowaries have none. A cassowary's wattle is usually blue, red, gold, purple, or white.

THE DANGEROUS DETAILS

Scientists think the casque may help guard the cassowary's head as it's running through the forest. Or it could help the bird make low sounds for other cassowaries to hear!

CASQUE

WATTLE

A CASSOWARY ISN'T BORN WITH A CASQUE. THE CASQUE BEGINS TO GROW WHEN THE BIRD IS ABOUT 1 OR 2 YEARS OLD.

TERRIBLE TOES

Some say the cassowary is the most dangerous bird in the world! It has scary **weapons** on its feet. Each foot has three toes. The inner toe has a supersharp claw that's 4 inches (10 cm) long!

When a cassowary comes face to face with an enemy, the bird may kick it. The cassowary's claw can cut, slice, and even kill another animal! Adult cassowaries don't have many enemies, but crocodiles, wild dogs, and large snakes called pythons are a few.

THE DANGEROUS DETAILS

Packs of wild dogs sometimes attack cassowaries. The birds need their special claws to **protect** themselves!

BIG, BIZARRE BODY

HARD CASQUE

WATERPROOF FEATHERS

SMALL WINGS

COLORFUL WATTLE

SUPERSHARP CLAWS

FLIGHTLESS, BUT FAST

Scientists think cassowaries may have lost the ability to fly over time because they didn't need to fly from their few enemies. They also don't need to fly to reach food. They're tall enough to get fruit on trees. They can wait for fruit to drop to the ground, too.

Cassowaries might not fly, but they can really move! They can run up to 30 miles (48 km) per hour. They can jump more than 6 feet (1.8 m) in the air. They can even swim!

THIS CASSOWARY AND ITS CHICK BATHE IN WATER. CASSOWARY CHICKS ARE BROWN OR TAN. THEY DON'T LOOK MUCH LIKE ADULT CASSOWARIES!

STAY AWAY!

Cassowaries may even use their fighting skills on each other! This bird likes to live alone in its territory. It may scare other cassowaries away by **stretching**, raising its feathers, making noises, and stamping its feet. If that doesn't work, it may kick!

Male and female cassowaries come together during **breeding** season. The female lays three to five eggs, but leaves the male to sit on them until they **hatch**. The father protects his young for months after the chicks are born.

CASSOWARY EGG

THE FATHER CASSOWARY WON'T EVEN LEAVE THE NEST TO EAT UNTIL THE EGGS HAVE HATCHED.

17

WHY THEY ATTACK

Most cases of cassowaries attacking people are linked to three causes. One is getting near eggs or chicks. Another cause is getting too close to a food source. But more than half of all attacks happen because cassowaries think people will feed them.

It's usually against the law to feed cassowaries, but people still do. Feeding makes the birds less shy. The birds then expect people to give them food, and when they don't—watch out! People have gotten broken bones and deep cuts from cassowary attacks.

CASSOWARY CAUTIONS

DON'T GO NEAR A CASSOWARY'S NEST OR CHICKS.

DON'T GET NEAR A CASSOWARY'S FOOD.

DON'T FEED CASSOWARIES.

DON'T GET NEAR A CASSOWARY AT ALL!

NO ONE HAS BEEN KILLED BY A CASSOWARY SINCE 1926, BUT THERE HAVE BEEN PLENTY OF **INJURIES!**

THE DANGEROUS DETAILS

In some parts of Australia, hungry cassowaries knock on windows and chase cars looking for food!

CARING FOR CASSOWARIES

Much of southern cassowaries' rainforest homes have been cut down, so these birds are in danger of dying out. Not much is known about the numbers of the other two species.

If cassowaries are dangerous to people, why should you care about them? They play an important role in nature. Southern cassowaries eat many kinds of fruit. When they poop, they spread seeds in other places so more fruit trees can grow. In fact, some seeds only grow if they pass through a cassowary's body. Cassowaries are incredible creatures!

THE SOUTHERN CASSOWARY IS CALLED A KEYSTONE SPECIES BECAUSE OF ITS IMPORTANCE IN SPREADING SEEDS.

THE DANGEROUS DETAILS

Fewer than 1,500 southern cassowaries remain in Australia. They're endangered, or in danger of dying out completely!

GLOSSARY

breeding: having to do with the process by which young animals are produced by their parents

hatch: to break out of an egg, or to break open

highland: an area where there are many mountains or where the land is high above the level of the sea

injury: harm or damage

lowland: an area where the land is at, near, or below the level of the sea and where there are not usually mountains or large hills

mineral: matter that is naturally formed under the ground

protect: to guard from harm

rainforest: a forest that receives a lot of rain and that has very tall trees

spongy: soft and full of holes, like a sponge

stretch: to spread arms and legs to look bigger or wider

weapon: something that is used for fighting or attacking someone or for defense when someone is attacking

FOR MORE INFORMATION

BOOKS

Hammond, Paula. *The Atlas of Endangered Animals: Wildlife Under Threat Around the World*. Tarrytown, NY: Marshall Cavendish, 2010.

Jenkins, Steve. *Never Smile at a Monkey: And 17 Other Important Things to Remember*. Boston, MA: Houghton Mifflin Books for Children, 2009.

WEBSITES

Birds—Cassowary
www.australiazoo.com.au/our-animals/birds/ratites/cassowary
Find out about the cassowaries at Australia Zoo.

Cassowary
animals.sandiegozoo.org/animals/cassowary
Read many other interesting facts about these cool birds.

Cassowary Facts
www.activewild.com/cassowary-facts/
Discover some quick facts about these beautiful big birds.

INDEX